This book belongs to ....

Mark the country you come from

This book was
made in India!

KATHA

THE CASE OF THE RUNAWAY CONTINENTS

geeta dharmarajan

art by joyita banerjee

THE INTRIGUING CLUES

In a world map, have you noticed how the bulge of Brazil fits snugly into the hollow of West Africa?

There are many other continents that fit together too, like pieces of a jigsaw puzzle.

This set geographers and scientists thinking ...

?

OTHER PUZZLING CLUES

Coral reefs need warm waters to stay alive. So why are there remains of them in the cold waters of Northern Hemisphere?

Coal and oil are formed when lush tropical forests fossilize for millions of years. So why do we find so much coal in North Europe? Or oil in Alaska?

Did tropical forests once cover these cold regions?

Often called "the rainforests of the sea", coral reefs are one of the most diverse ecosystems on Earth. In India, the Andaman and Nicobar Islands have the biggest coral reef formation.

FOSSIL EVIDENCE

AFRICA

SOUTH AMERICA

Cynognathus
(Triassic land reptile)

Mesosaurus
(Freshwater reptile)

Why do certain animals in South America share ancestors with animals that live only in Africa?

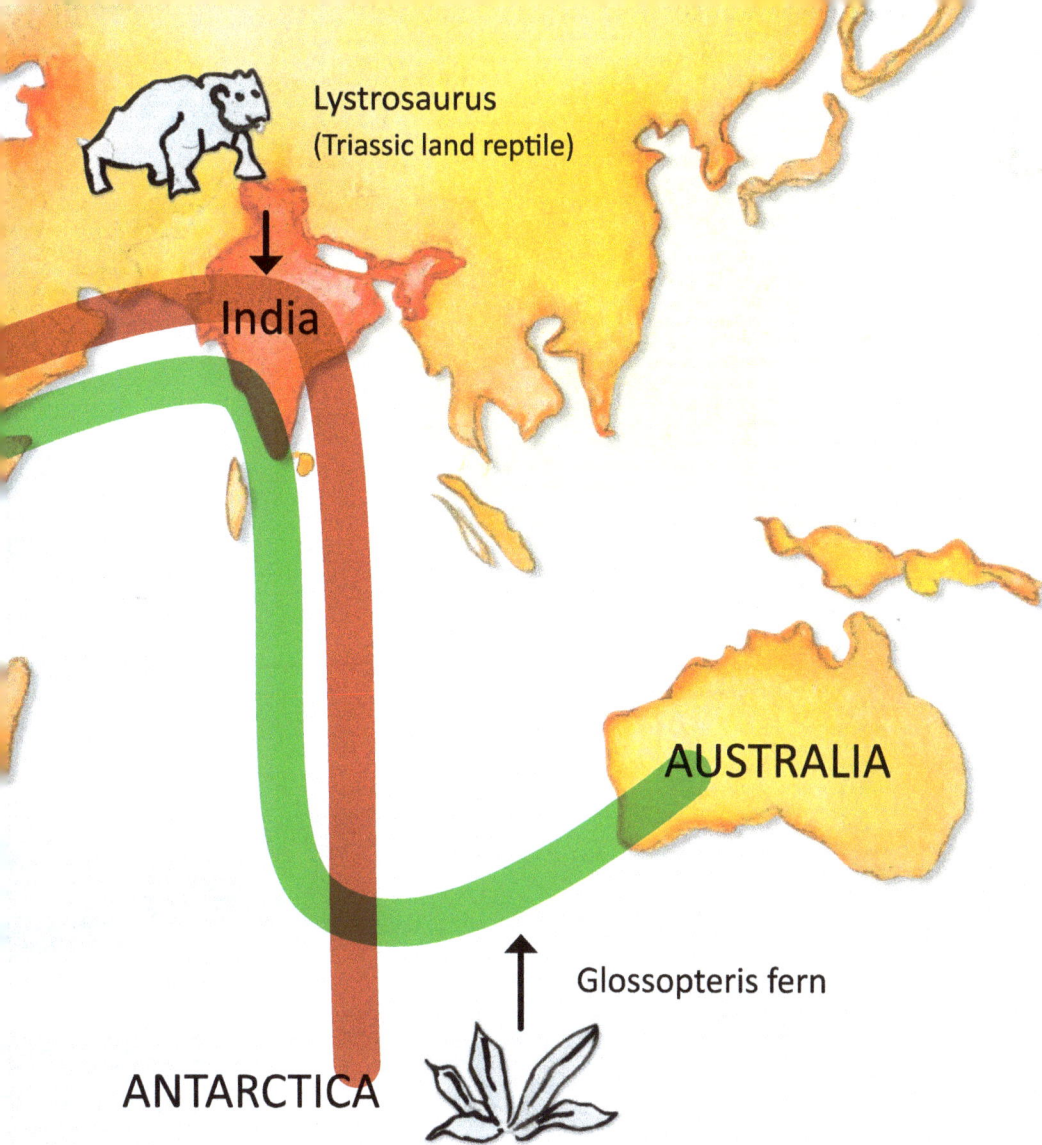

Lystrosaurus
(Triassic land reptile)

India

AUSTRALIA

Glossopteris fern

ANTARCTICA

While carbon dating rock samples from different coastlines of an ocean, geologists found that their age and pattern proved that they might have belonged to the same rock.

BUT HOW – with all that sea in between?

The only possible answer to all these vexing questions is: Earth must have been one huge landmass and all the continents must have been together. They then moved apart over a period of time. Scientists call this phenomenon the **continental drift.**

200 MILLION YEARS AGO »»»»»» 180 MILLION YEARS AGO »»

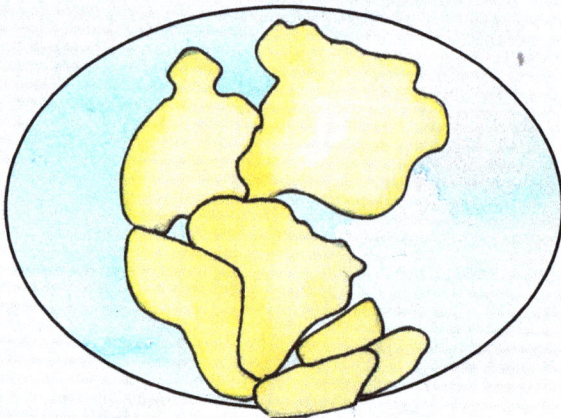

The supercontinent of Pangaea

The breakup of Pangaea

If you could zoom back 200 million years or so, you would find just one solid mass of land, named Pangaea by geologists.

65 MILLION YEARS AGO 〉〉〉〉〉〉〉〉 PRESENT

Continents drift further apart   Continents as seen today

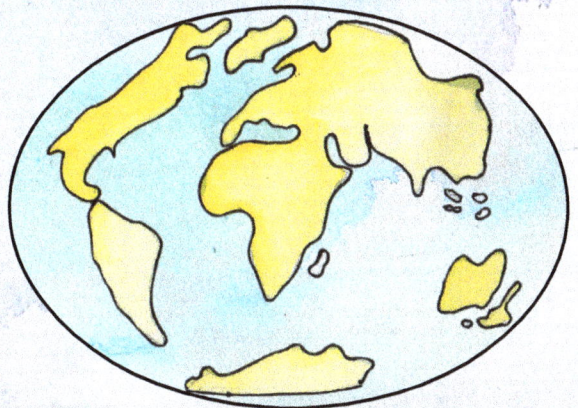

LOOK! NO WHEELS

About 140 million years ago, the solid mass of land slowly drifted apart to form Gondwanaland and Laurasia. Thousands of years passed, the continents moved and reached where they are today. And they are still moving!

Gondwanaland was named by Austrian geologist, Eduard Suess, after the Gondwana region of Central India (from Sanskrit "gondavana," forest of the Gonds).

How?

Why?

You would get tired asking "why" if you did not know that the continents are not fixed to Earth as if to a solid ball.

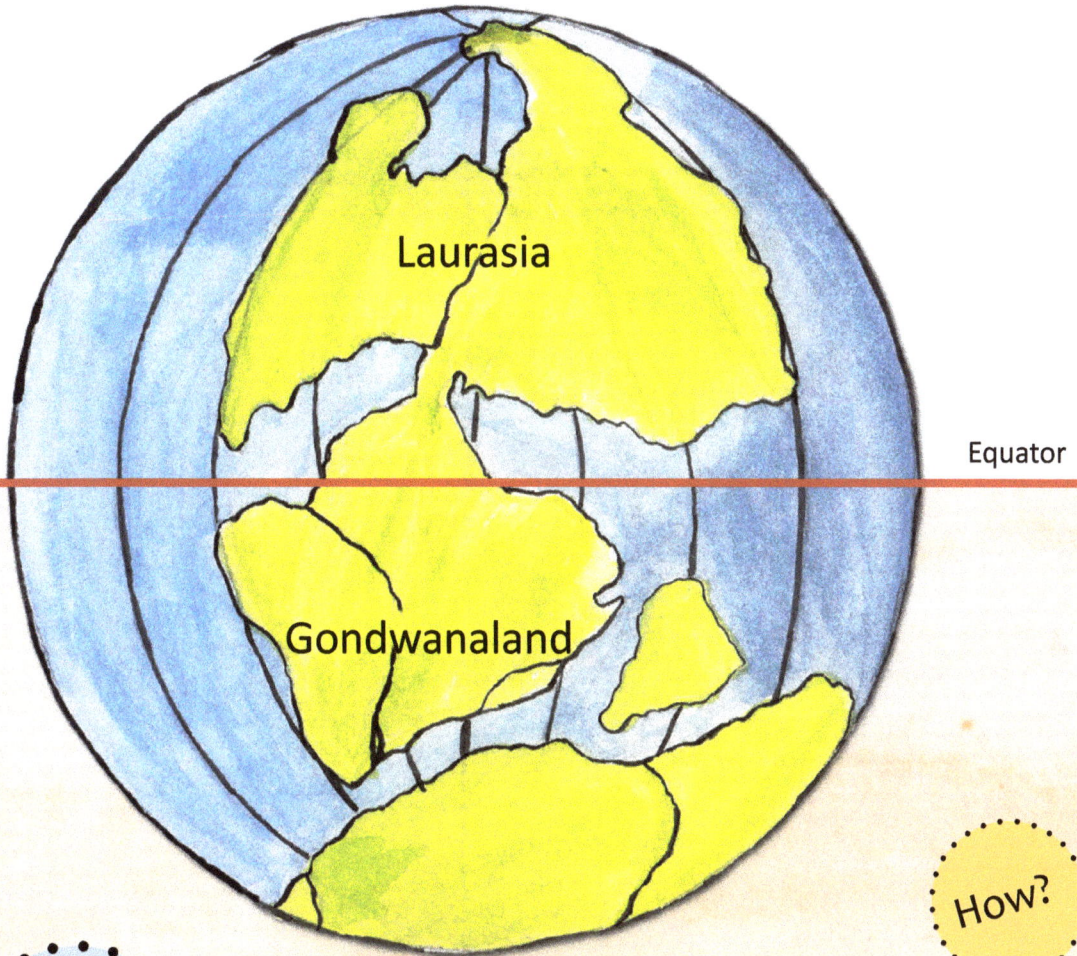

Laurasia

Equator

Gondwanaland

Still moving?

How?

How?

WATCH OUT EARTH'S CCCCCR

Cracks! Impossible, you might say. But ...

"Without a cracked earth, we cannot explain many of the mysteries of our Earth," said Alfred Wegener, father of the continental drift theory, whose pioneering ideas laid the groundwork for the modern science of plate tectonics.

THE SHOCKING EVIDENCE

The whole outside layer of Earth, including the land and the seabed, is a hard crust.

This crust floats on the mantle, a layer of molten rock.

The crust is a thin layer compared to the size of Earth. It is no thicker than the skin of an apple, as compared to the apple.

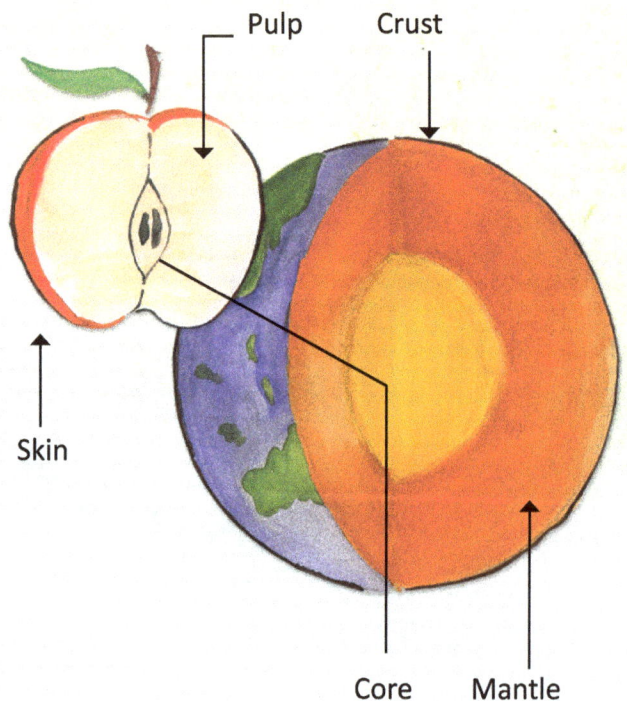

Pulp

Crust

Skin

Core

Mantle

Ocean →

Stationary or moving plate

Oceanic crust

Lithosphere

Rising magma

Oceanic crust ↓

Lithosphere

Hotspot

Asthenosphere

Continent

Stationary or moving plate ←

Continental crust ↓

Lithosphere

Rising magma

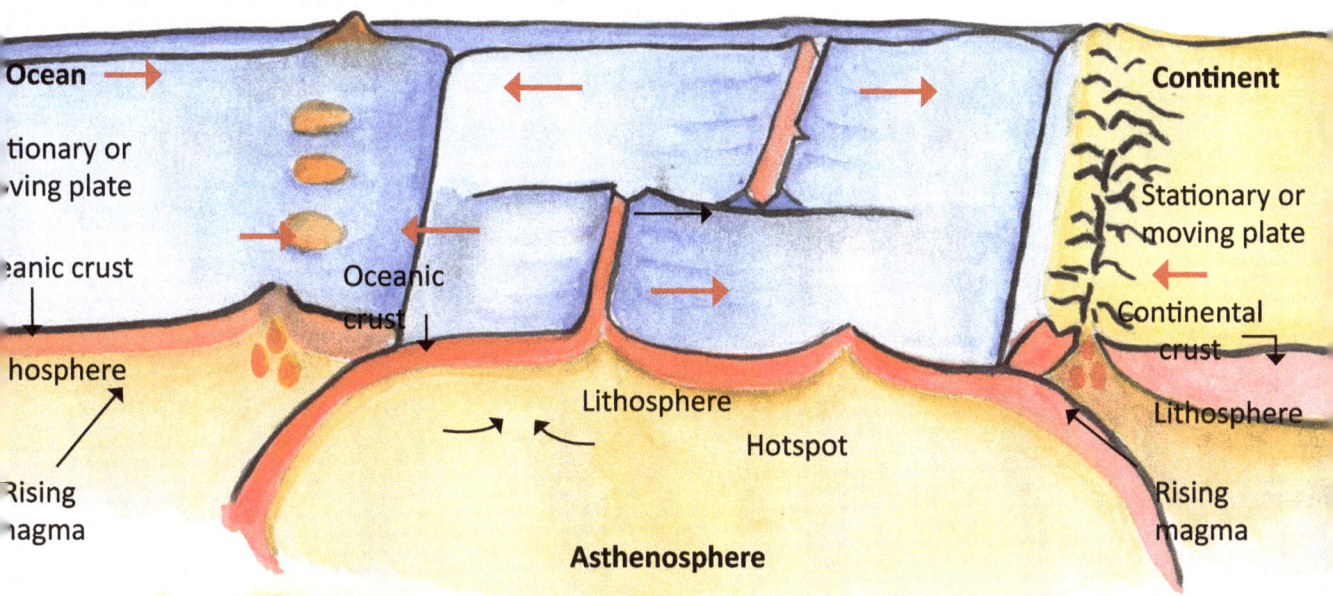

The crust is not a complete shield for the inside of Earth either. Like a cracked eggshell, it is divided into several plates or bits of crust with cracks or areas of weakness where two or more plates meet.

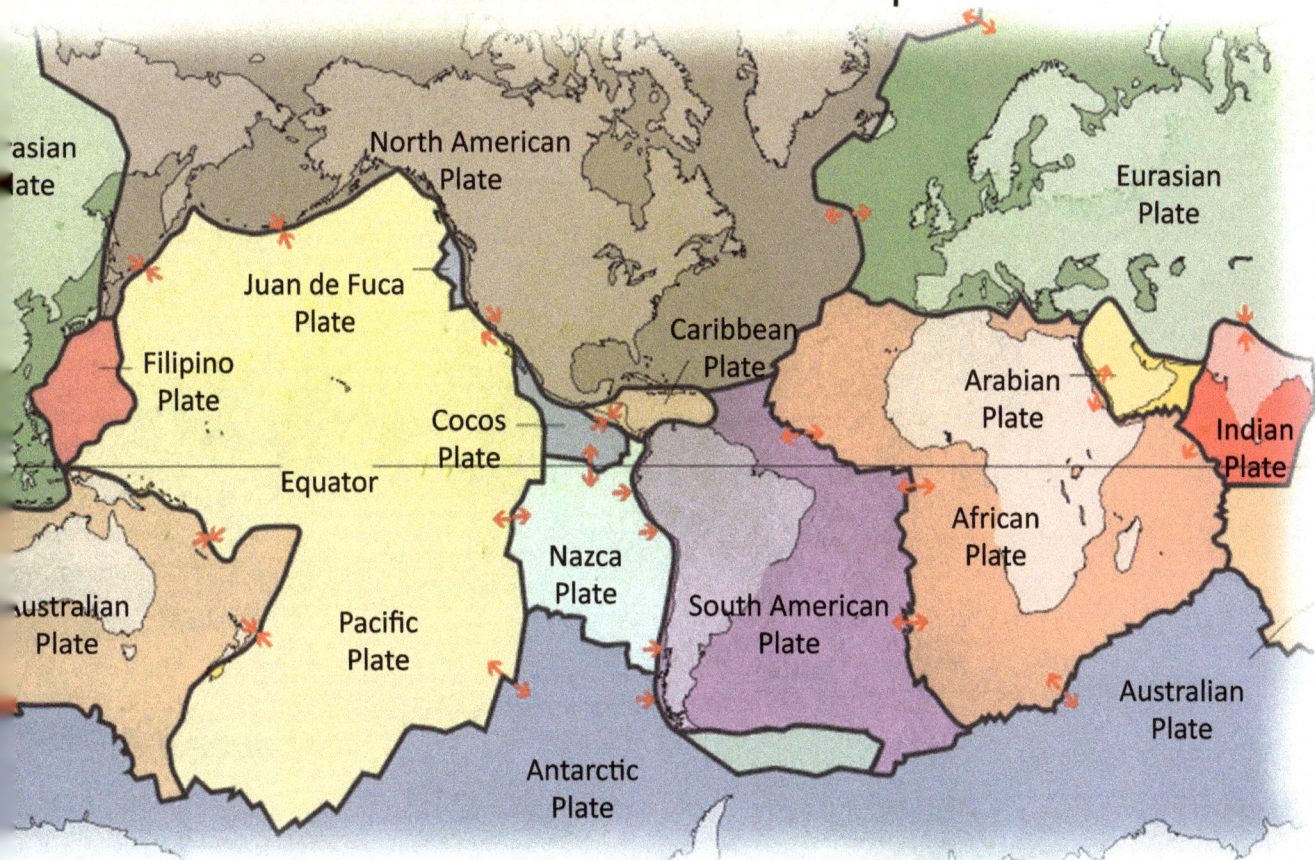

Eurasian Plate

North American Plate

Juan de Fuca Plate

Filipino Plate

Caribbean Plate

Arabian Plate

Eurasian Plate

Indian Plate

Cocos Plate

Equator

African Plate

Australian Plate

Nazca Plate

South American Plate

Pacific Plate

Australian Plate

Antarctic Plate

NOT JUST HOT AIR

You know that hot air rises, well, so does hot rock! Melted rocks, below Earth's crust, are called **magma.**

When strong currents of magma reach the cracks, the currents squeeze through them like toothpaste from a tube. This mostly happens when the crust is thin.

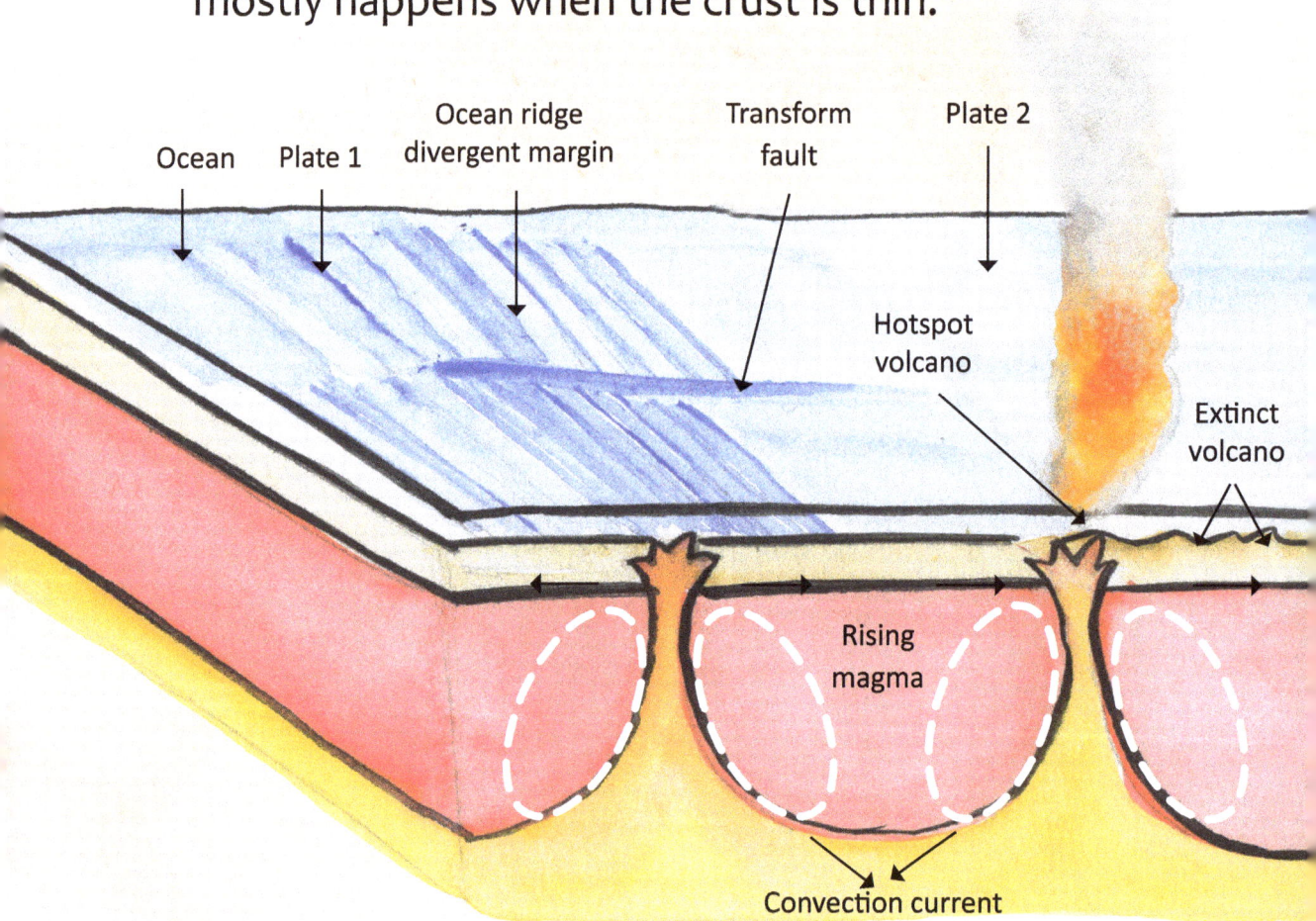

Ocean

Plate 1

Ocean ridge divergent margin

Transform fault

Plate 2

Hotspot volcano

Extinct volcano

Rising magma

Convection current

But when these cracks appear on the land, they usually cause violent earthquakes and volcanic eruptions.

Earthquakes can happen anywhere but they mostly affect the areas along the plate boundaries, the fault zones, or along the cracks that appear in the middle of the plates.

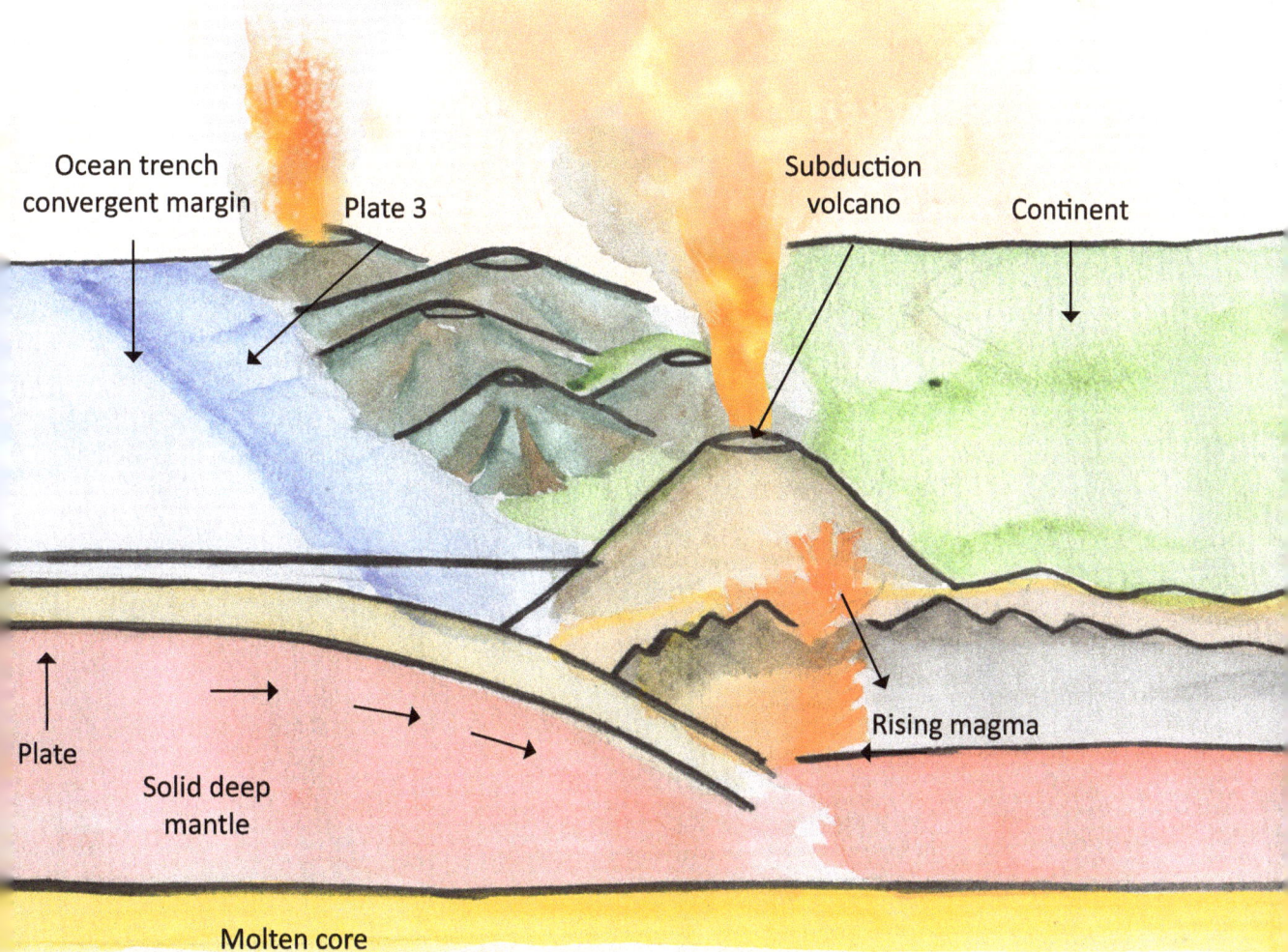

Ocean trench convergent margin

Plate 3

Subduction volcano

Continent

Rising magma

Plate

Solid deep mantle

Molten core

HIGHER THAN THE HIMALAYAS

Do you know that there is a mountain range bigger, wider and taller than the Himalayan range? And it is mostly the underwater Mid-Atlantic ridge! It is about 60,000 km long and several hundred kilometres wide. And it is growing wider at the rate of 2.5 cm per year!

This underwater ridge, discovered in 1956, runs along the crack in the crust of Atlantic Ocean and goes all the way to the Gulf of California.

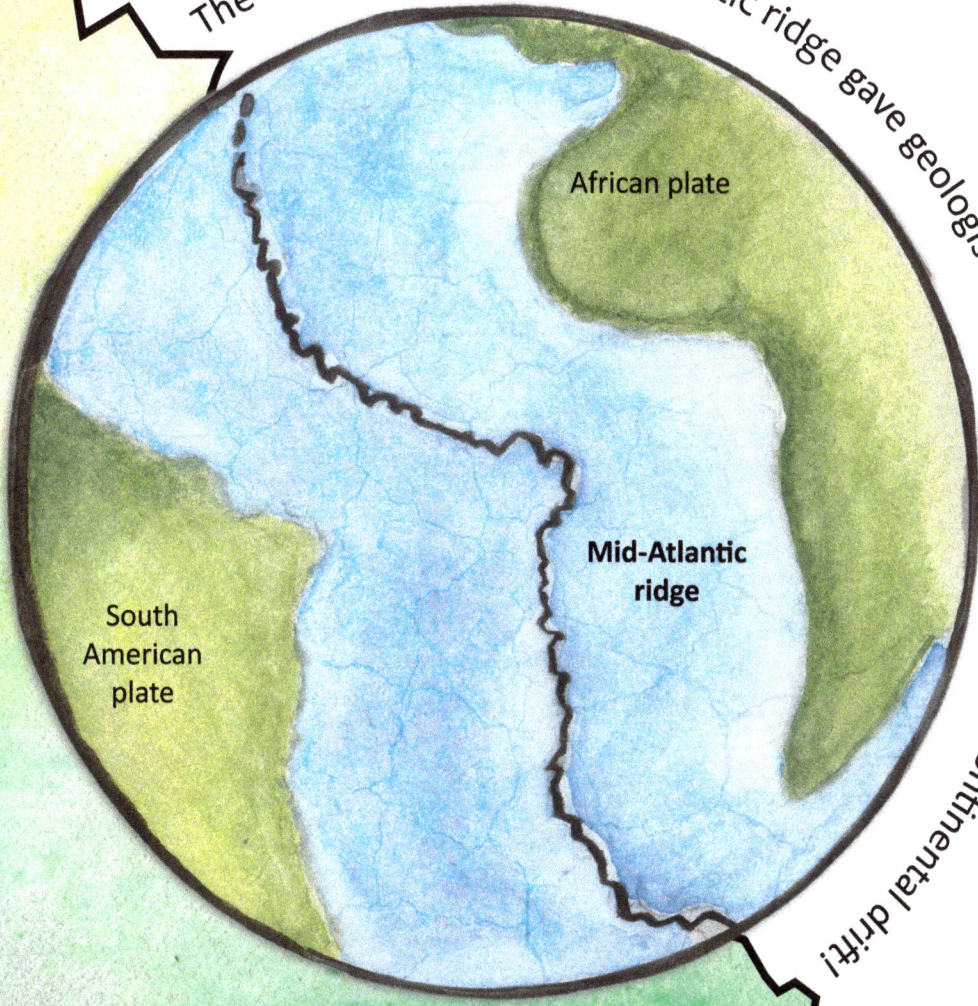

The discovery of the Mid-Atlantic ridge gave geologists the first solid evidence of continental drift!

African plate

South American plate

Mid-Atlantic ridge

About two third of Earth's surface is beneath the ocean. Studying the ocean bed and the ridge system, geologists found that as the magma squeezes out it becomes solid, forming a new layer of land.

Growing Ocean Floor!

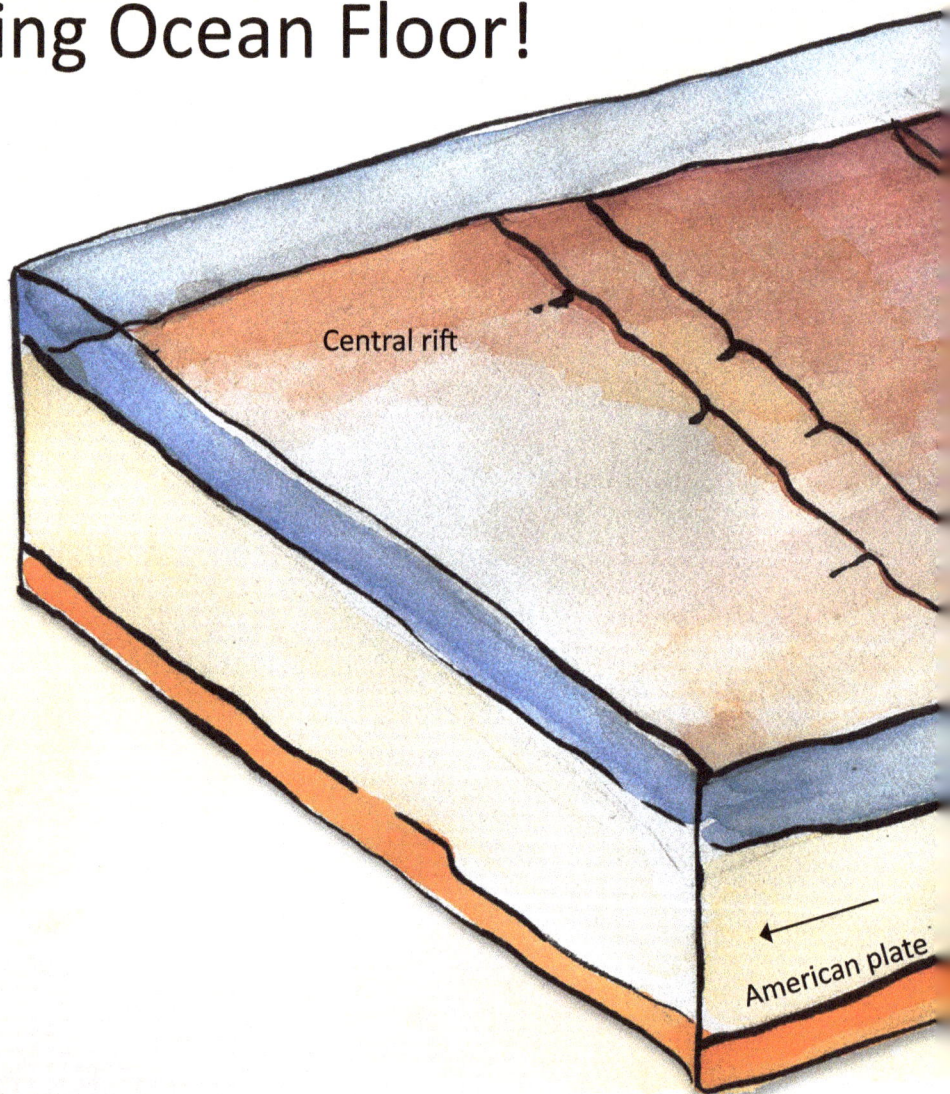

Central rift

American plate

When the next wave of lava comes out, it pushes this old lava further away from the crack. This makes the ocean floor grow. That is why the tectonic plates are always shifting.

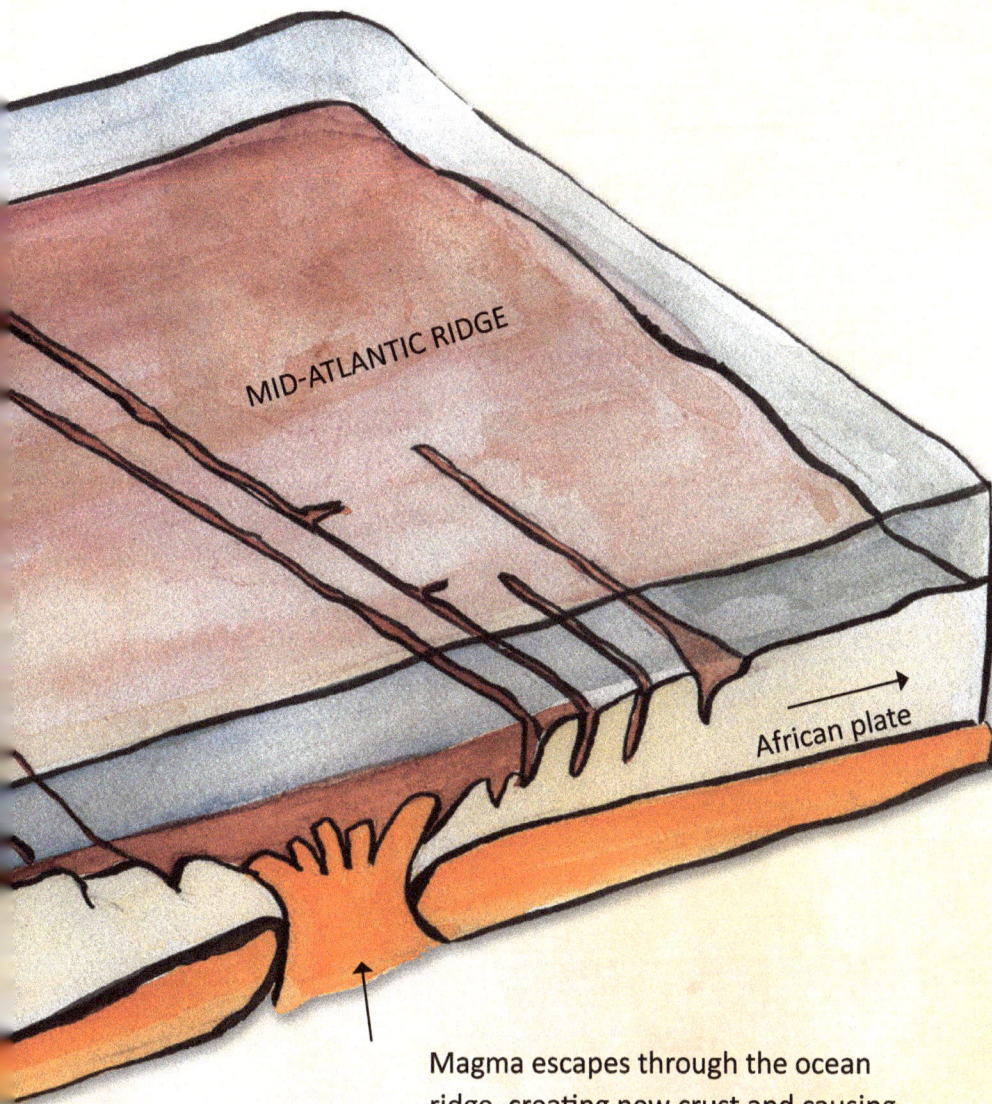

MID-ATLANTIC RIDGE

African plate

Magma escapes through the ocean ridge, creating new crust and causing the ocean floor to expand.

TAKEN FOR A RIDE!

When the plates move, they collide with other plates or sometimes slide one under the other. When this happens, Earth changes. Mountains get built. Ocean floors grow. Volcanoes erupt and earthquakes happen. And naturally, the continents that are on the crustal plates get taken for a ride!

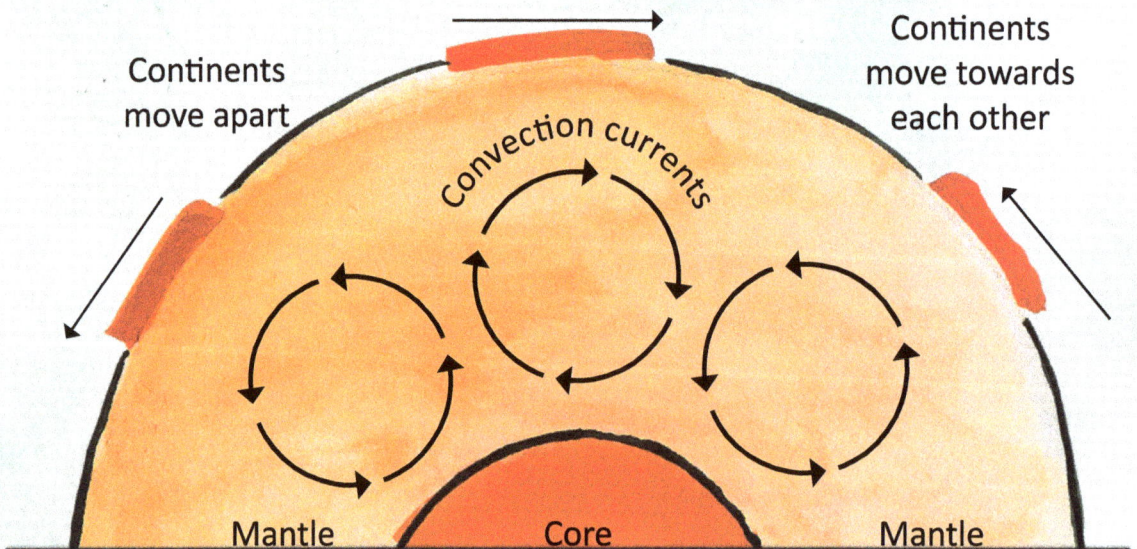

Continents move apart

Continents move towards each other

Convection currents

Mantle

Core

Mantle

EURASIAN PLATE

INDIA

10 million
years ago

Today

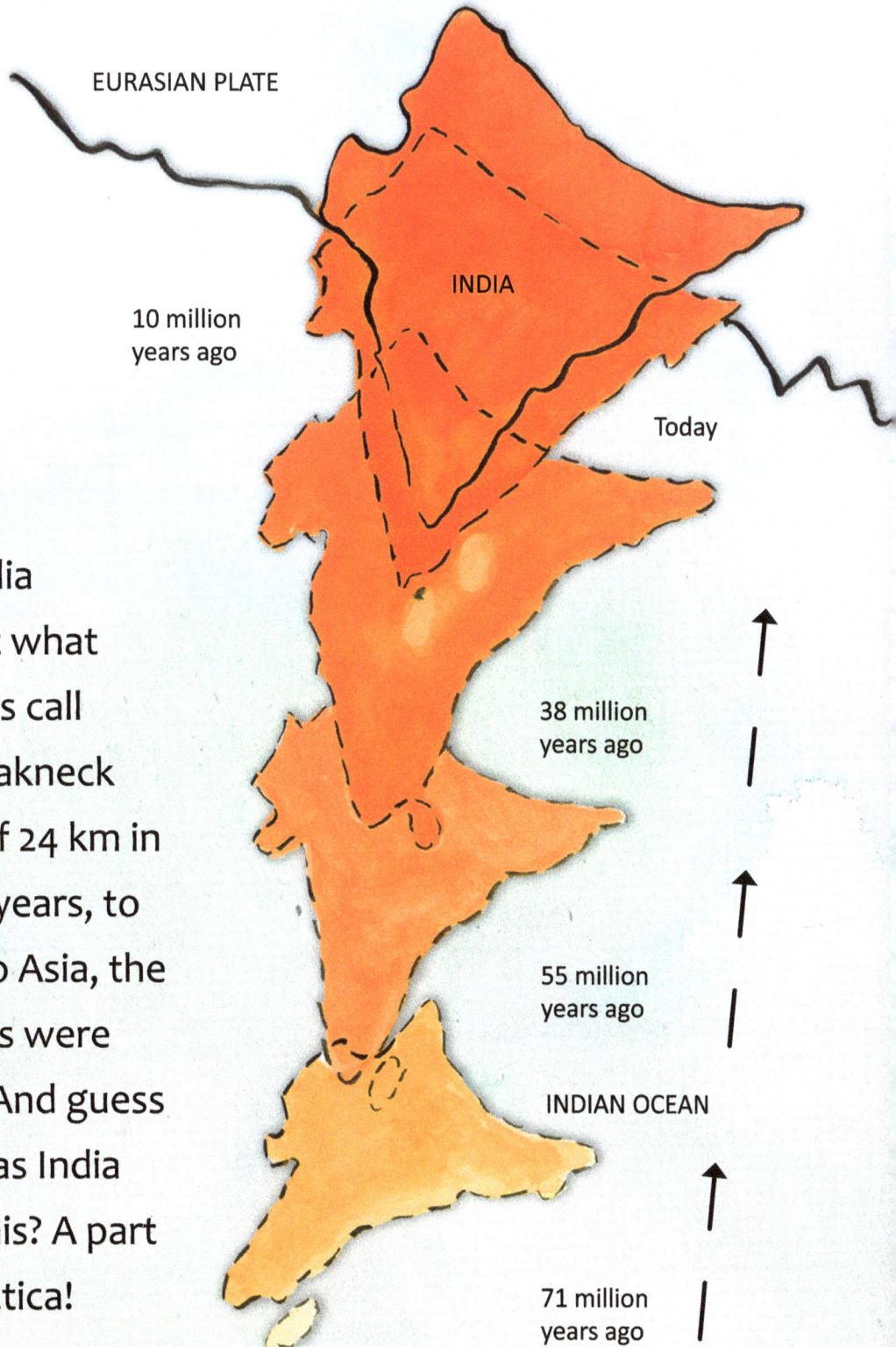

When India
moved at what
geologists call
the "breakneck
speed" of 24 km in
a million years, to
crash into Asia, the
Himalayas were
formed! And guess
where was India
before this? A part
of Antarctica!

38 million
years ago

55 million
years ago

INDIAN OCEAN

71 million
years ago

IS THE EARTH GETTING BIGGER?

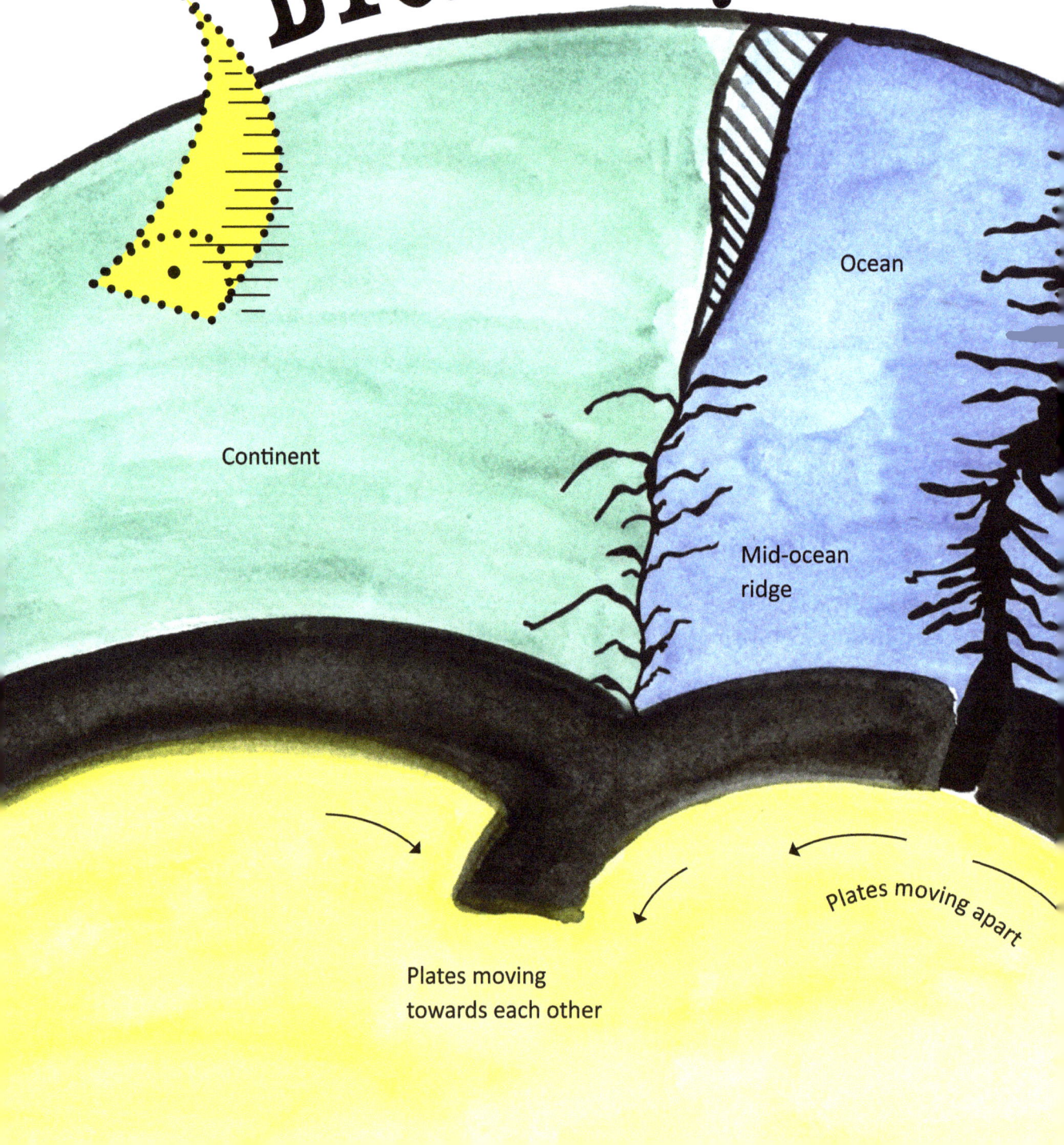

Ocean

Continent

Mid-ocean ridge

Plates moving apart

Plates moving towards each other

Shouldn't Earth grow in size to accommodate new land formations? Then why does it not?

The reason why it doesn't is quite simple, it's because of **trenches**, the cracks in between the plates.

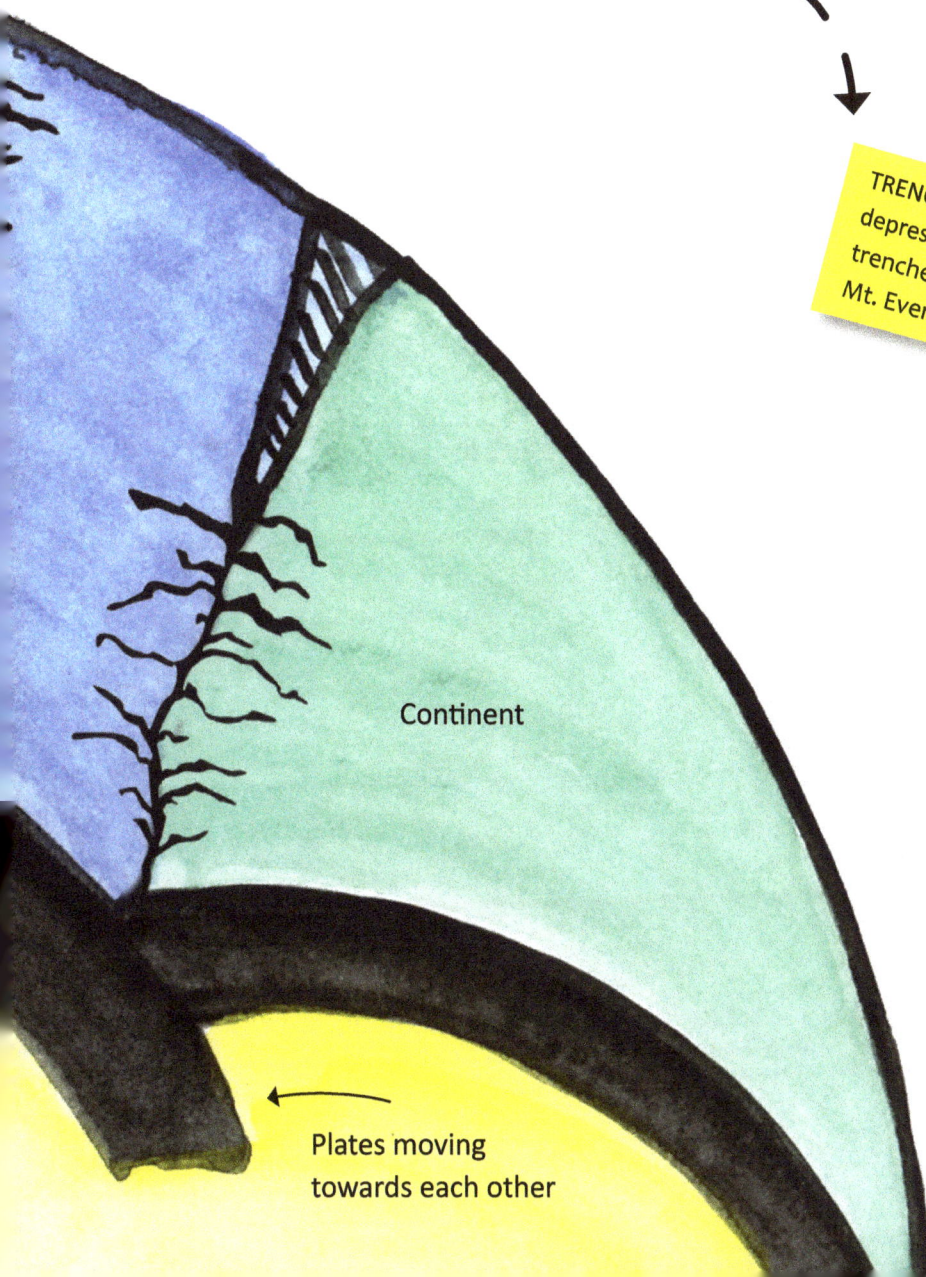

TRENCHES are long, narrow and deep depressions on the ocean floor. Some trenches are 35,000 ft deep! By contrast Mt. Everest is only 29,029 ft high!

Continent

Plates moving towards each other

The Ring of Fire

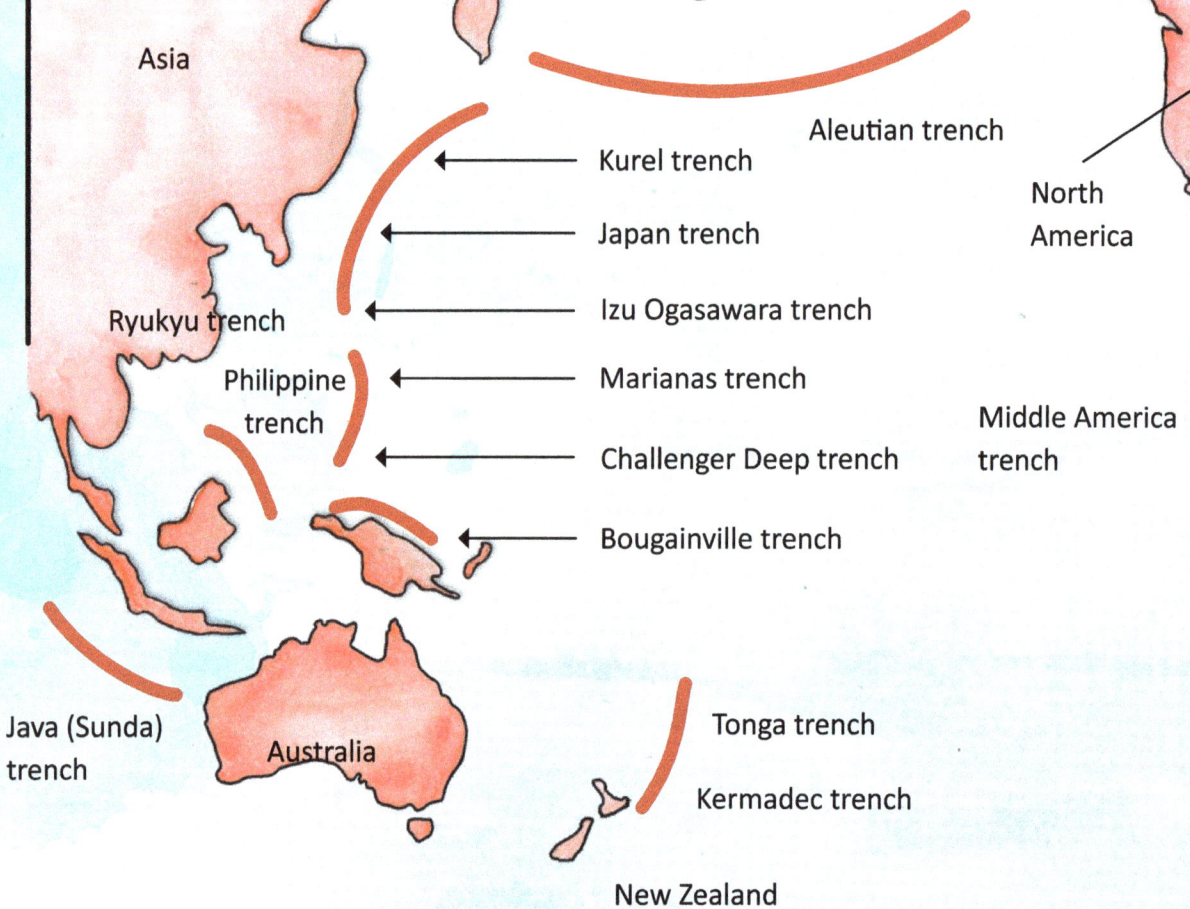

Asia

Kurel trench

Japan trench

Izu Ogasawara trench

Ryukyu trench

Philippine trench

Marianas trench

Challenger Deep trench

Bougainville trench

Aleutian trench

North America

Middle America trench

Java (Sunda) trench

Australia

Tonga trench

Kermadec trench

New Zealand

Nowadays, the motion of the tectonic plates is studied using latest computers and remote sensing satellite data.

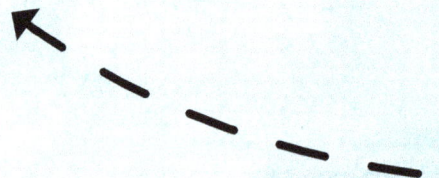

Puerto Rico trench

South
America

Peru-Chile
trench

Chile

When scientists were mapping the ocean ridge system, they found that the edges of the Pacific Ocean had deep trenches. They named this belt of trenches "the Ring of Fire." This is because it has 452 volcanoes! More than 75% of the world's volcanoes lie here.

Here, the downward pull of the magma sucks the crust back into the mantle, making land sink into Earth and disappear!

Some scientists think that while the Atlantic Ocean is growing wider, the huge, gentle Pacific Ocean is progressively shrinking and, perhaps, in 500 million years it would all but disappear!

These extremely slow but constant changes in Earth's continental crust follows a timeline. Scientists call it the

supercontinent cycle.

One complete cycle takes 350 to 500 million years. During this time, the huge landmasses or supercontinents break up or merge.

Scientists speculate that right now we are in the middle of a cycle. They predict that within the next 250 million years, the continents will smash together again to form a new single supercontinent.

NEXT SUPERCONTINENT
200 - 250 million years

TODAY

PANGAEA
300 - 200 million years ago

**PANNOTIA/
GREATER GONDWANA**
600 million years ago

(partial supercontinent)

RODINIA
1.1 billion - 760 million
years ago

COLUMBIA (NUNA)
2 - 1.8 billion years ago

KENORLAND
2.5 billion years ago

UR
3 billion years ago

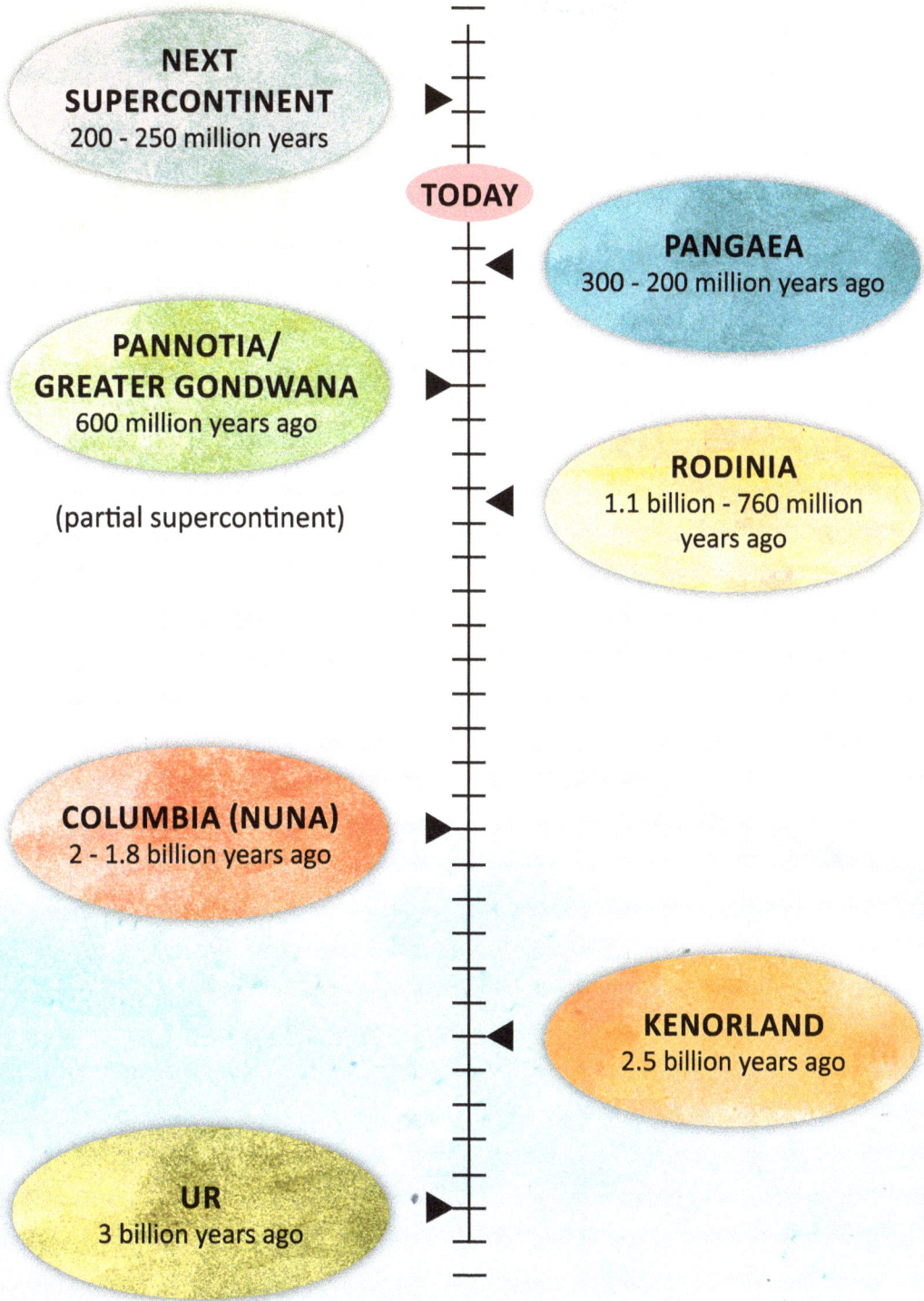

TIMELINE OF SUPERCONTINENTS

Imagine you're on Earth 250 million years from now! Our planet has changed drastically just as it did in the time of dinosaurs. All the continents have come together to form a new Pangaea. You can now walk from Africa to America!

Earth is still home to a bewildering array of life forms. Yet apart from a few mysterious fossils,

there is no trace that we, humans, ever existed!

Geeta Dharmarajan loves writing stories for children. She was one of the editors of *Target*, a magazine for children and *The Pennsylvania Gazette*, the magazine of the University of Pennsylvania. She has been awarded the prestigious Padma Shri in 2012, for her distinguished service in the fields of Literature and Education.

Joyita Banerjee graduated from Pearl Academy, Delhi and works with Katha as a graphic designer. *Old Man Who Would Not Listen* is her first illustrated book for children. Joyita also loves to travel and take photographs.

WEBSITES REFERRED TO FOR CONTENT

http://whatonearth.olehnielsen.dk/tectonics/ridges.asp (Last accessed on 26 November 2013)

http://www.cotf.edu/ete/modules/msese/earthsysflr/plates1.html (Last accessed on 26 November 2013)

http://www.cotf.edu/ete/modules/msese/earthsysflr/geotime.html (Last accessed on 26 November 2013)

http://www.pbs.org/wgbh/aso/tryit/tectonics/ (Last accessed on 26 November 2013)

http://science.nasa.gov/science-news/science-at-nasa/2000/ast06oct_1/ (Last accessed on 26 November 2013)

http://www.scotese.com/futanima.htm (Last accessed on 26 November 2013)

http://www.yale.edu/ynhti/curriculum/units/1991/6/91.06.05.x.html (Last accessed on 26 November 2013)

http://www.enchantedlearning.com/subjects/dinosaurs/glossary/Contdrift.shtml (Last accessed on 26 November 2013)

http://en.wikipedia.org/wiki/Continental_drift (Last accessed on 26 November 2013)

http://en.wikipedia.org/wiki/Plate_tectonics (Last accessed on 26 November 2013)

WEBSITES REFERRED TO FOR IMAGES

South America fits into Africa and fossil distribution: http://curriculum.kcdistancelearning.com/courses/ENVSCIx-AP-U10/a/unit05/apes_5.c.4.html (Last accessed on 26 November 2013)

Ring of Fire: http://pubs.usgs.gov/gip/dynamic/fire.html (Last accessed on 26 November 2013)

Cracking Earth: http://www.freewebs.com/morganisrupert/photos.htm (Last accessed on 26 November 2013)

The apple and the structure of Earth: http://library.thinkquest.org/17457/platetectonics/1.php (Last accessed on 26 November 2013)

India's movement: http://college.holycross.edu/projects/himalayan_cultures/2006_plans/hkaiter/The_Himalayas.htm (Last accessed on 26 November 2013)

Convection currents: http://www.platetectonics.com/book/page_4.asp (Last accessed on 26 November 2013)

Future world: http://www.photosfan.com/future-world/ (Last accessed on 26 November 2013)

Supercontinents timeline: http://polymath07.blogspot.in/2008/02/middle-aged-earth.html (Last accessed on 26 November 2013)

Convergent boundary: http://scullyproject.wikispaces.com/Convergent+Boundary (Last accessed on 26 November 2013)

Mid-ocean ridge: http://www.daviddarling.info/childrens_encyclopedia/Dig_a_Hole_to_China_Chapter2.html (Last accessed on 26 November 2013)

KATHA

First published © Katha, 2014
Copyright © Katha, 2014
Text copyright © Geeta Dharmarajan, 2014
Illustrations copyright © Joyita Banerjee, 2014
All rights reserved. No part of this book may be reproduced or utilized in any form without the prior written permission of the publisher.
ISBN 978-93-82454-15-1
E-mail: marketing@katha.org, Website: www.katha.org

KATHA is a registered nonprofit organization devoted to enhancing the joys of reading amongst children and adults. Katha Schools are situated in the slums and streets of Delhi and tribal villages of Arunachal Pradesh.
A3 Sarvodaya Enclave, Sri Aurobindo Marg
New Delhi 110 017
Phone: 4141 6600 . 4182 9998 . 2652 1752
Fax: 2651 4373

Ten per cent of sales proceeds from this book will support the quality education of children studying in Katha Schools.
Katha regularly plants trees to replace the wood used in the making of its books.

GET TO KNOW EARTH BETTER!

Triassic is a geologic period from about 250 to 200 million years ago during which reptiles flourished.

Glossopteris is the largest and best-known type of the extinct order of seed ferns known as Glossopteridales.

Ridge is a long, narrow and continuous stretch of hills or mountains.

Subduction zone is a region of Earth's crust where two tectonic plates meet.

Subduction volcanoes are volcanoes above subduction zones.

Lithosphere (about 100 km thick) is the outer, solid part of Earth, which includes the crust and uppermost mantle.

Plate tectonics is a scientific theory that describes the large-scale motions of Earth's lithosphere.

Asthenosphere (about 180 km thick) is the squashy part of Earth just below the lithosphere.

Can you trace the Ring of Fire?

www.ingramcontent.com/pod-product-compliance
Lightning Source LLC
Chambersburg PA
CBHW041634040426
42447CB00020B/3492